THE WORKBOOK:
SIMPLY COMMON-CENTS:
THE HOW OF MENTAL STABILITY

MY WORDS, YOUR REALITY ™

COPYRIGHT @2018 BY: RONALD W. ALSTON, SR.

For added information about purchasing books or booking Ronald W. Alston, Sr., for speaking and training engagements write:

Ronald W. Alston, Sr.

Printed by: Create-Space Publications an

Independent Publishing Platform

Available through Amazon.com

Blog: drronalston.com

Cover Design: Shon Burnett: (order@vizion2life.com)

Edited By: Kelly Alston Muhammad, B. S.

ISBN: 13: 978-1985784574

ISBN: 10: 1985784572

TABLE OF CONTENT

<u>**INTRODUCTION**</u>

Here is your workbook, an off-shoot and reference guide to my crowd-pleaser, 'Simply Common-Cents, the Discipline of Uncommon Reasoning.'

This (workbook) guide takes you step-by-step through the process of navigating through your 'stuck-points' in a way that can be mind-opening, while providing you with the privilege of behavioral discovery, or finding out why you act the way you do under any given condition. The way you elect to act, is a direct result to how you have elected to think.

If you're anything like me, I never liked the idea of NOT knowing because knowledge is power, and that same knowledge can set you free from yourself. Many of us are prone to get in our own way, so this workbook is your personal map that directs you to ideas that redefine your thinking resolutions by subjective intent because you're the focal point!

Simply Common-Cents, the Workbook, is illustrative by nature, and quietly challenges you to get to know yourself a great deal better. Your behavioral patterns can now be a vehicle that identifies clearly what you need to work on to control that anger, remove that shame or guilt, and equips you with symbolic 'MIND CONTROL.'

PART I
THE IMPORTANCE OF INTEGRITY

Lesson 1:

Integrity is Your Truth

Integrity, the other word for honesty, and a more common term that relates to truth, must be your circle between the square. The square is what surrounds you, and the circle represents all of who you are being the good, bad, and the indifferent. As easy as this may sound, the square is where your influences arise. All of us are influenced by others from family and friends, to those who are considered antagonists.

The point being made here is that we adopt behavioral patterns that aren't necessarily intended but are absorbed internally nonetheless. Influences overtime quickly becomes a part of who we are even before we realize it ourselves. If these influences have a negative charge, the likelihood of these influences alter, modify, and derail the truth about yourself.

One of the most difficult things to do is to admit being flawed!

Possessing the ability to recognize these negative mental charges due to the personality influence of others, it will be necessary to examine these behavioral distinctions to avoid a character assault that you suffer. The flaws that perhaps you have will forever be referred to as 'stuck-points.' These stuck-points are character flaws, personality inconsistencies, coupled with a damaged belief system. Many of our flaws originate from our past, and when gone untreated, these flaws only get worse. This workbook will enable you to identify, and progressively follow a resolution pattern that will assist you in finding that solution.

> *You must be hungry for more than the temporary pleasures of life. Mental healing comes with your own persistence! Your own truth will be your salvation, therefore, find your Peace!*

PART 2

IDENTIFYING YOUR STUCK-POINTS

Lesson 2:

What is a Stuck-Point?

Stuck-Points are character flaws that you refuse to acknowledge, or simply ignore. These character flaws have become a learned experience or a decision that you made when you decide to adopt and maintain.

A stuck-point doesn't have to be negative in and of its definition, but it can also be something considered to be positive but obsessive. An over indulgence of a character trait can be that one thing that unnerves someone else. A simple explanation of a stuck-point is that thing about you that gnaws at the gut of someone, but even you can be the blame. Being **disliked,** being **arrogant,** being a **braggart,** appearing **greedy or jealous,** or expecting an **excessive amount of attention** are stuck-points that are readily seen by others, but ignored by you. If you're a person who no one wants to be around, or avoids, there is a reason for it, and you need to find out why.

> **"When you are inspired, your mind transcends its limitations as your conscientiousness now expands." Dr. Wayne Dyer**

To readily identify your stuck-points it's essential to follow these three (3) steps.

> **1. OBSERVATION**
> **2. INTERPRETATION**
> **3. APPLICATION & RESOLVE**

The following page will ask several questions of you that will mirror your ability to self-detect. This will test your integrity and your willingness to self-indict.

Lesson 2:

YOUR OWN SUBJECTIVITY

Explain what you have learned in lesson (2)

____

____

____

____

____

____

____

____

____

____

____

____

____

____

____

____

____

____

<u>Continue to explain what you learned in lesson 2.</u>

<u>Question 3, List Your Stuck-Points</u>

<u>LIST YOUR TOP THREE</u>

<u>ADD MORE IF YOU CHOOSE</u>

1 ______________________________________

2 ______________________________________

3 ______________________________________

4 ______________________________________

5 ______________________________________

6 ______________________________________

7 ______________________________________

8 ______________________________________

PART 3

WELL-ADJUSTED THINKING

Lesson 3:

YOUR BALANCED THOUGHT PROCESS

When an individual is persistent in his/her thinking the meaning of that thought is interpreted by a sound evaluation of all circumstances that you, the subject, is faced with mastering. When anything is balanced, the scales of life are in sync with everything about your being. When your thinking is balanced the control of your behavior is imminent.

Once you have identified your stuck-points the clarity that you are hopefully seeking will soon come to pass. When there is transparency, you have balance and when balance exists, what is born to that is called *transformation.* The human psyche has now become this photograph into your spirit that allows an interaction of mind, body, and spirit.

The next page will be another worksheet that will allow you to define what 'having balance' means to you. When anything is written by you the thought that follows is a keener understanding of what is real but held shielded within your mind because you elect NOT to give it up.

Lesson 3: Worksheet/Questionnaire

1. Explain how you see the model of 'Balanced Thinking?'

____

____

____

____

____

____

____

____

____

____

____

____

____

____

____

____

____

____

____

____

____

____

____

Lesson 3: Questionnaire Continued

2. Is the idea of having the ability to balance your thoughts important to you? If so, WHY? If not, why? Be clear on which you choose.

____

____

____

____

____

____

____

____

____

____

____

____

____

____

____

____

____

____

PART 4:

CHALLENGING QUESTIONS

YOUR INTRODUCTION TO CHALLENGING QUESTIONS

This section will take you down a path of explaining the mental tools you elect to choose regarding how you can navigate through your thoughts. These decisive thought processes will direct you in every way by helping you to determine the fundamental steps to your healing from the inside out. For every action, there is a reaction, and how you react will also determine how quickly you can resolve new and old 'stuck-points.' Remember, everything has a cause and affect factor, if you can find the cause and then examine it thoroughly, you're on your way to healing that which has plagued you for many years.

> ***You can't give away what you don't have at your disposal!***
> ***In a world of make believe, your realities could be skewed!***
> ***Every challenger was once a contender!***

In your book, 'Simply Common-Cents,' there are ten (10) anecdotes that will help you pilot through your thought patterns. For each stuck-point that you identify there is a solution available that will assist you in negotiating the reason and the resolve for that stuck-point. As you will find, many of the long-ranging problems that you have had are merely habits which you have grown accustomed and the need to change has not met your immediate purpose. In many instances, these 'stuck-points' have become YOUR convenience.

So, here are a few of those *mind anecdotes* that I need for you to explain that are associated with those stuck-points you previously selected in lesson 2. As you answer these questions explain why or why not.

CHALLENGING QUESTIONS: QUESTIONNAIRE

1. *What does the **Evidence For** mean as that relates to your stuck-points? (This query would apply for every stuck-point that you have selected.)*

____

____

____

____

____

____

____

____

____

____

2. What does the **Evidence Against** mean?

____

____

____

____

____

3. What is considered a **Habit** that relates to your stuck-points?

5. What is your stuck-point that is based on **Feelings or Facts?**

4. What is a stuck-point that is **Routine or Truth Rendering?**

6. Is your stuck-point **Excessive or Overstated?**

____

____

____

____

____

____

____

____

____

____

____

____

____

____

____

____

____

____

____

____

____

7. Is the source of your stuck-point **Dependable? Why or why? not?**

8. Is your stuck-point **Low vs. High Probability?** If so, why? Pick one.

____

____

____

____

____

____

____

____

____

____

____

____

____

____

____

____

____

____

____

____

____

____

____

____

9. Are there **Unrelated Factors** attached to your stuck-point? Why or why not?

10. Are the **Interpretations** of your stuck-point not accurate?
Why or why not?

____

____

____

____

____

____

____

____

____

____

____

____

____

____

____

____

____

____

____

____

____

PART 5:
RATING YOUR STUCK-POINTS

Lesson 4:

How to RATE your Stuck-Points.

Once you have made your character trait assessments and ***specifically*** identified your stuck-points, you need to rate those stuck-points from 0-100%. A hundred percent would be the absolute worse as to the severity of each of your stuck-points and how it affects your behavior. Of course, the lower the number the more control you're gaining over your emotions to alter, modify, and hopefully dismiss that emotional breach.

Rating, like anything else is subjective and depends solely on how honest you can be with your emotions and yourself. What's important here is that you fully understand your assessment of any given 'stuck-point' and then clearly discuss these thinking solutions by writing about them. Hence, utilize the tool of writing your 'Impact Statement.'

Rating is good because it allows you to see your progress from beginning to end. Periodically, go over your written evaluations and match them with your IMPACT STATEMENT and make note of any improvement or not.

PART 6:

WRITING YOUR IMPACT STATEMENT

Lesson 5:

Writing Your Impact Statement

Your impact statement is quite frankly your *TRUTH STATEMENT*. When you begin to compose this statement refer to the lessons that you have covered thus far. This statement will identify your stuck-points one at a time as you then cover how your stuck-point has affected your life, and perhaps the life or lives of others.

As your identified stuck-points should number more than one or two, each one is rated separately and recognized in standings of priority. This statement is a candid admission that you have flaws and that you're NOT PERFECT IN ANY WAY. This will be determined by identifying your abnormal or undesirable behavior where you can now begin to understand why people see you in such a negative way where you aren't even aware of it yourself. The fact that you aren't aware of it is because you have never been told by anyone that you are difficult to know and deal with on any level. These character traits are ways in which people judge you, and the first thing they all expect once they encounter you.

Please note, as I mentioned earlier, that a stuck-point isn't always an emotion that is negative, but it can also be an obsession that works for you but drives someone else CRAZY. Obsession is an over-action that is recognized by how you talk and how you act out. The troubling nature of obsession is that you can't control it or you're not aware of it. If the obsession is made known to you, the acceptance of it will determine your level of maturity and the means that you select to remedy that obsessive stuck-point.

BEGIN WRITING YOUR STUCK-POINTS ONE AT A TIME AND IN THE ORDER OF PRIORITY. WORK UNTIL YOU HAVE COMPLETED ALL OF THEM. WRITE TO UNDERSTAND!

STUCK-POINT # 1. (ENTER YOUR STUCK-POINT)

____

____

____

____

____

____

____

____

____

____

____

____

____

STUCK-POINT # 2. (ENTER YOUR STUCK-POINT)

STUCK-POINT # 3. (ENTER YOUR STUCK-POINT)

SUMMARY CONCLUSION

Before you have reached the end of this work in progress ask yourself this question; "did I get it?' Do I really understand what I've done to get closer to who I am in the present, and what it will take for me to reach a much higher thinking platform? If you're not there yet, perhaps you need to reread the book, go over and answer the questions held within this workbook, and then KEEP trying! This must be the end all to your mental discomfort and the only way to approach that measure is to reread and actively participate if you wish to heal.

You need to capture this model below unconditionally by carefully determining what it is about yourself that needs to be changed. Remember, a habit is formed following (3 weeks) of effort.

IDENTIFY STUCK-POINT	MIND NAVIGATION	ALTERNATIVE
YOUR ISSUES (s)	*Your Thinking Process*	*Your Resolution for Healing*

MY WORDS
OPEN MIND
YOUR REALITY